GRAIN FREE MADE EASY

21 INCREDIBLE RECIPES TO HELP YOU LOSE WEIGHT AND STAY HEALTHY

J.S. West

I0482283

[FREE eBook LIMITED offer]

As a "Thank You" note to your interest in my recipe books, I'd like to offer my latest eBook for FREE up to 1000 amazon kindle downloads.
There aren't many left so grab your free copy now!

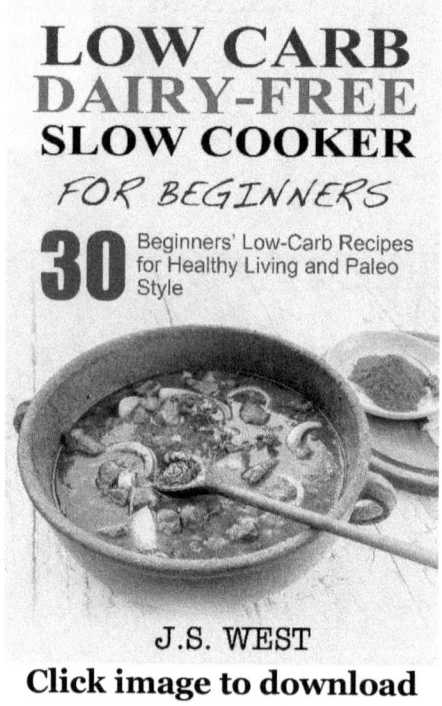

Click image to download

presentation of the information is without contract or any type of guarantee assurance.

The trademarks that are used are without any consent, and the publication of the trademark is without permission or backing by the trademark owner. All trademarks and brands within this book are for clarifying purposes only and are the owned by the owners themselves, not affiliated with this document.

Table of Contents

Introduction

I want to thank you and congratulate you for downloading the book, "Grain Free Made Easy: 21 Delicious Recipes to Help You Lose Weight and Stay Healthy".

This book contains proven steps and strategies on how to shed extra weight and keep your body healthy by removing grains from your diet.

The recipes in this book are designed with the beginning cook in mind, and the beginning dieter, too! There's no need to be concerned about having to eat bland, boring foods, or about having to spend hours in the kitchen if you want to eat anything that tastes good. With this book here to help, you'll be preparing tasty grain-free dishes in no time at all!

Thanks again for downloading this book, I hope you enjoy it!

Chapter 1 - What Is Grain Free?

Chances are that you have probably heard the term "grain free" in some form before. This is an over-arching term that can be applied to several different varieties of diet plans, all of which have merit. To begin with, the low-carb Atkins diet and its other carb-counting cousins can be at least labeled as "low grain" diets. This is because grains tend to be one of the leading sources of carbohydrates in any given diet, so eliminating carbs automatically reduces grains significantly.

There are other diets, however, that fit into the grain-free category even better than Atkins does. A celiac diet, also much more commonly referred to as gluten-free dieting, is also by its very nature a grain-free diet. In recent years, people have come to realize the devastating effects of gluten on the human body—even on bodies that don't have celiac disease! The less gluten you eat in a day, the better your body will feel and look. And once again, grains are a leading culprit when it comes to gluten.

Last but not least, the paleo diet is also a grain-free style of eating. The paleo diet has become very popular recently, and paleo practitioners have reported significant weight loss and increased overall bodily health—particularly in the area of digestion. The paleo diet is grain-free by nature because the foremost rule of paleo is to eat what early hunter-gatherers would have eaten. They would not have known to eat grain, and would not have grown it, so it therefore would not have been a staple of their diets—and so it must be avoided.

As each of these diets proves, it pays to eliminate grains! Removing grains from daily consumption will lead to weight loss and a much healthier, more vibrant you. So, are you ready to learn more?

Chapter 2 - Myths about Grain Free Dieting

It takes too much time to cook food that tastes any good.

Don't worry! There are tons of delicious thirty minute recipes that are readily available to grain-free dieters. As grain-free eating becomes more and more popular, the number of tasty and easy recipes just continues to grow! And if you cook with a slow cooker, you have the option to set your food to cook and then go about your daily business without worrying about it for a few hours. How much easier can it get?

It is too difficult to avoid grains.

While it is true that grains are present in many different types of food, you simply have to learn to read labels and you will be just fine. Make sure to look for flour, wheat, barley, yeast, malt, semolina, spelt, germ, or rye on any ingredient label. When in doubt, buy something in its most natural form (raw meat or veggies, for example) and prepare it yourself at home!

It is too expensive to cook at home.

It's much more expensive to eat out all the time—even fast food!—than it is to prepare your foods at home! In fact, most of your ingredients can be bought in bulk and frozen until you need to prepare them. Meat, vegetables, and even some fruits can readily be found in large bags for freezing, and at very affordable prices, too! Don't be afraid to shop around and use coupons when you need to, but don't worry. Home cooked meals are very inexpensive.

Chapter 3 - Tips for Grain Free Dieting

Stock Your Kitchen

It is vital to the success of your grain-free diet for you to keep your kitchen fully stocked and equipped. You are sure to give up easily if you don't have the ingredients and utensils on hand that you will need in order to prepare the recipes in this book. Keep various types of flour, milk, eggs, meat, fruits, and vegetables on hand, and don't forget your oils and spices, too! As for utensils, remember to have pots, pans, knives, a whisk, bowls, and possibly a slow cooker available for easy use.

Make Meal Plans

If you make yourself a couple of lists each week, your diet will go much more smoothly! First, make a list of the meals you plan to eat each day of the week. Then, write down a grocery list including everything you will need to prepare those meals. Make sure to check your pantry and refrigerator stocks to see what you already have, and what might need replacing! Then, stick to your list when you go shopping. You'll be far less tempted to eat foods you shouldn't!

Stick To The Basics

Remember that you will always need a few basics on hand in your kitchen, and don't stray from the grain-free options that are available to you. For flour substitutes, try almond flour or arrowroot powder; coconut flour is also a great option, especially for baking. Opt for olive oil, bacon fat, ghee, and coconut oil instead of butter, and in place of cow's milk, use almond or coconut milk. Sweeten your foods with honey or maple syrup instead of sugar or artificial sweeteners. And reach for sea salt instead of regular table salt!

Chapter 4 - 7 Breakfasts

Pumpkin Blueberry Muffins

The unique combination of flavors in these muffins will leave you craving more!

1/3 cup maple syrup

1/3 cup pumpkin puree

1/4 cup melted coconut oil

1 tsp vanilla extract

3 whisked legs

1/4 cup and 2 tbsp coconut flour

1 tbsp pumpkin pie spice

1/2 tsp baking powder

1/2 tsp baking soda

1/4 tsp salt

2 tbsp honey

2 cups blueberries

1 tsp lemon juice

2 tbsp coconut cream

Preheat oven to 350 degrees Fahrenheit.

In a large bowl, combine syrup, puree, oil, vanilla, and eggs.

In a separate bowl, combine 1/4 cup flour, pumpkin pie spice, baking powder, baking soda, and salt.

Pour dry ingredients into wet and combine thoroughly.

Pour muffin batter into a baking sheet; bake for 35 minutes.

Meanwhile, place blueberries in a small pot on the stove over medium heat and cook until just bursting.

Add coconut cream, honey, and lemon juice, and stir to combine thoroughly.

Remove from heat; stir in remaining coconut flour, then let sit 5 minutes to thicken.

Pour mixture on top of crust; bake for 15 minutes more.

Let cool 10 minutes.

Slice and serve.

Banana Bread

This classic breakfast is great for kids and adults both.

2 bananas, mashed

1/2 cup coconut sugar

1/2 cup almond milk

2 eggs

1 tsp vanilla

1 tsp cinnamon

1/4 tsp nutmeg

2 cups almond meal

2 tbsp honey

1/2 cup walnut pieces

1/4 tsp baking soda

Preheat oven to 350 degrees Fahrenheit.

Combine all ingredients in a large bowl.

Mix thoroughly, either by hand or with an electric mixer.

Spread into a loaf pan; optionally, top with more banana slices.

Bake for 40 minutes.

Let cool 10 minutes.

Serve.

Breakfast Sandwiches

Sometimes, you just can't beat a breakfast sandwich!

1/2 cup tapioca flour

1 cup almond flour

1/4 cup coconut flour

1/2 tsp baking powder

1/2 tsp baking soda

2 whole eggs

4 egg whites

2 tbsp melted bacon fat (or ghee)

Breakfast toppings of your choice (scrambled eggs, bacon, sausage, veggies, etc.)

Preheat oven to 350 degrees Fahrenheit.

Sift together all flours with baking powder and baking soda in a large bowl.

In a separate large bowl, beat egg whites until frothy, then pour egg whites into dry mixture; combine thoroughly.

Add whole eggs and bacon fat; whisk thoroughly.

Refrigerate batter for 30 minutes.

Scoop out batter onto baking sheet to form four biscuits.

Bake for 18 minutes, then let cool

Top with toppings of choice.

Serve.

Faux Breakfast "Burrito"

The whole family is sure to love this twist on the classic breakfast burrito!

4 thick slices of deli ham

1/4 cup chopped spinach

1/4 cup chopped black olives

1/4 cup chopped tomato

1/4 cup chopped bell pepper

8 eggs

Salsa or guacamole to taste

Cook vegetables over medium high heat until sautéed to desired doneness; add spinach in the last 3 minutes to wilt slightly, or eat raw.

Whisk eggs in a small bowl.

Pour eggs over vegetables and scramble gently over medium-low heat.

Remove scramble from pan.

Place egg mixture into each slice of ham and roll tightly.

Add ham rolls to skillet and cook over medium heat for a few seconds per side to crisp edges.

Serve with guacamole and salsa to taste.

Ricotta Chard Muffins

Serve up a healthy portion of calcium-rich muffins with this simple recipe.

1/2 cup chopped onion

1 tbsp olive oil

1 minced clove of garlic

2 cups ricotta cheese

8 cups chopped Swiss chard

3 eggs

1/4 cup shredded Parmesan

1 cup shredded mozzarella

1/8 tsp ground nutmeg

1 pound mild sausage

Preheat oven to 350 degrees Fahrenheit.

Cook onions and garlic in olive oil in a skillet over medium heat for 7 minutes.

Add chard and cook for 5 minutes to soften stems and wilt leaves.

Add nutmeg, then remove from heat and let cool.

While cooling, beat eggs together in a large bowl with all cheeses.

Stir in cooked greens mixture.

Press sausage into a pie tin evenly.

Pour over filling evenly.

Bake for 35 minutes or until firm.

Let cool 5 minutes.

Serve.

Chocolate Peanut Butter Smoothie

If you're looking for a quick breakfast that can be easily stored and transported, look no further than this sweet treat!

1/2 cup chocolate almond milk

1 frozen banana

2 tbsp fat-free Greek yogurt

1 tbsp cocoa powder

2 tbsp peanut butter

1 tsp honey

Add all ingredients to a blender.

Blend on high until smooth.

If you prefer a thinner smoothie, add more almond milk.

Serve.

Apple Pie On-The-Go

For all the delicious flavors of apple pie and none of the mess, try these easy bars!

1/2 cup raw macadamia nuts

2 cups pitted dates

1/2 cup dried apples

2 tbsp melted coconut oil

1/4 cup raw almonds

2 tbsp cinnamon

Add dates, macadamia nuts, almonds, and apples to a food processor and pulse on high until chunky.

Add to a mixing bowl with remaining ingredients.

Mix by hand to coat thoroughly.

Flatten mixture onto parchment paper evenly, then place in refrigerator and chill for at least 1 hour.

Slice and serve.

Chapter 5 - 7 Lunches

Basil Salad

Enjoy the favor of basil alongside your spinach in this easy lunch salad.

1/2 diced yellow onion

1 tbsp coconut oil

2 diced tomatoes

1 package fresh basil

4 handfuls spinach

Melt coconut oil in a small skillet over medium-high heat.

Cook onions for 7 minutes in coconut oil.

Add tomatoes and cook for 1 minute more.

Add spinach and basil and cook for 1 minute more.

Serve salad warm.

B "L" T Salad

Use arugula in place of the lettuce in this salad for a healthier alternative!

8oz diced pre-cooked boneless skinless chicken thighs or breasts

4 diced slices of bacon, pre-cooked

4 tbsp peperoncini brine

4 sliced peperoncini peppers

4 cups arugula

1 diced avocado

1 diced tomato

1/4 cup toasted sunflower seeds

Place arugula in a large bowl and pour over peperoncini brine.

Add bacon and chicken; toss to coat everything.

Toss in avocado, tomato, and sunflower seeds.

Serve.

Cantaloupe Salad

This cool summertime salad is perfect with the accompanying dressing!

4 tsp honey

3 tbsp lime juice

2 tbsp olive oil

1/2 tsp sea salt

1 avocado

1 cantaloupe

Whisk lime juice together in a large bowl with oil, honey, and salt.

Dice cantaloupes and peel skin off.

Peel avocados and dice.

Toss cantaloupes and avocados in dressing.

Serve.

Italian Salad

This is a slightly more in-depth salad that's great for a lunch gathering.

3 tbsp olive oil

2 tbsp lemon juice

1 minced clove of garlic

1/2 tsp dried oregano

1/4 tsp red pepper flakes

1 bunch kale, washed

1/2 pound diced hard salami

1/2 cup peperoncini peppers

1/2 cup cherry tomatoes

4 marinated artichoke hearts

1/4 cup toasted sunflower seeds

1/4 cup green olives

4 picked red onion slices

In a small container with a lid, such as a mason jar, combine olive oil with lemon juice, garlic, oregano, and red pepper flakes.

Cover and shake to combine.

Slice kale leaves thinly and discard stems.

Toss kale with dressing to coat thoroughly.

Top with remaining ingredients as desired.

Serve.

Sardine Salad

Even those who don't like sardines are sure to be pleasantly surprised by this salad!

1 diced yellow summer squash

3 diced tomatoes

1 diced stalk of celery

1/4 cup sauerkraut

1 chopped head of Romaine lettuce

1 cup shredded cabbage

6oz canned sardines in oil, chopped

2 diced avocados

1 tbsp lime juice

1 tbsp balsamic vinegar

1/4 tsp sea salt

1 tsp Dijon mustard

Toss all ingredients in a large bowl to combine flavors thoroughly.

Optionally, chill for 30 minutes before serving.

Serve.

Southwest Salad

This salad is inspired by the flavors of salsa.

4 diced roma tomatoes

1 bunch chopped cilantro

1 diced chili pepper

1 diced yellow onion

1 diced avocado

1 tbsp olive oil

1/4 tsp sea salt

Toss tomatoes in a large bowl with cilantro, chili pepper, and onion.

Add olive oil and salt; toss again to coat.

Serve topped with diced avocado.

Tuna Salad

Mix up this classic tuna salad and serve it over Romaine lettuce for a tasty lunchtime treat.

1/2 cup diced artichoke hearts

6oz canned tuna, drained

1/2 cup diced sun dried tomatoes

1/2 cup chopped pitted kalamata olives

3 tbsp olive oil

1 chopped roasted red pepper

2 tbsp lemon juice

1 tsp Dijon mustard

2 tbsp chopped basil leaves

1/4 cup chopped fresh parsley

2 tbsp chopped mint leaves

Flake tuna into a large bowl.

Add olives, artichokes, tomatoes, and red pepper; stir to combine thoroughly.

In a small container with a lid (such as a mason jar), add lemon juice, olive oil, mustard, and herbs; close and shake thoroughly.

Toss dressing with tuna mixture.

Chill for 30 minutes.

Serve.

Chapter 6 - 7 Dinners

Red Pepper Salmon

This delicious and very simple salmon recipe is inspired by the flavors of Italy.

3 tbsp lemon juice

2 red bell peppers

1/2 tsp sea salt

1 tbsp honey

2 tbsp olive oil

1 diced onion

24oz salmon filets

6oz sliced shiitake mushrooms

Minced parsley, to taste

Preheat oven to 350 degrees Fahrenheit.

Place peppers in a baking dish; roast for 20 minutes.

Let cool, then remove stems and seeds.

Place peppers into a blender with honey, salt, and lemon juice; blend on high until smooth.

Cook onion for 1 minute in olive oil in a skillet over medium heat.

Add mushrooms; cover, turn head to medium-low, and cook 10 minutes.

Turn oven to 500 degrees Fahrenheit.

Place fish on a metal baking sheet, skin side down.

Turn temperature down to 275 degrees Fahrenheit and place the salmon on the lowest rack of the oven.

Roast for 13 minutes.

Serve salmon on top of pepper puree, topped with mushrooms and parsley.

Turkey Chili

Serve up a comforting bowl of warm chili with this heart-healthy, grain-free recipe!

2 quarts chicken stock

4 roasted poblano chili peppers

2 diced onions

2 tsp ground cumin

3 diced carrots

1 tsp dried oregano

1 tbsp arrowroot powder

1/2 tsp sea salt

1 tbsp minced cilantro

1 tbsp water

Place turkey, poblanos, onions, carrots, and stock in a slow cooker.

Cover and cook for 8 to 12 hours on low.

Add oregano, cumin, and salt; stir to combine flavors.

Whisk arrowroot into water in a small bowl, then stir into slow cooker.

Cover and cook on low for 1 hour more to thicken.

Serve topped with cilantro.

Piccata

The savory flavors in this tasty cod-based dish are sure to please!

1/2 cup almond flour

1-1/2 pounds cod

1/2 tsp sea salt

5 tbsp olive oil

1/2 tsp Italian seasoning

5 tbsp grapeseed oil

1/4 cup lemon juice

1 cup chicken stock

1/4 cup capers in brine

1/4 cup chopped fresh parsley

Slice cod into six equal pieces.

Combine flour with salt and Italian seasoning.

Dredge fish pieces in flour mixture.

In a skillet over medium-high heat, warm olive oil and 2 tbsp grapeseed oil; brown cod pieces for 3 minutes per side in skillet.

Add lemon juice, capers, and chicken stock to the same skillet and deglaze the pan by scraping the browned pieces into the sauce.

Cook until reduced by half.

Whisk in remaining grapeseed oil.

Serve cod topped with sauce and sprinkled with parsley.

Shrimp Curry

Enjoy this meal when you want a very light, flavor-packed dinner!

4 cloves garlic

4 tbsp olive oil

1 chopped onion

2 tsp minced fresh ginger

1/2 cup pureed tomatoes

1/2 tsp cumin

1/2 tsp turmeric

1/2 tsp coriander

1 chopped bunch cilantro

3 tbsp lime juice

1 pound peeled large shrimp

Heat oil in a large skillet over low heat.

Add onion and garlic and cook for 10 minutes.

Add ginger, tomatoes, coriander, cumin, and turmeric, and simmer for 5 minutes more.

Add shrimp and cook 5 minutes; flip and cook 5 minutes more.

Stir in cilantro and lime juice.

Serve.

Kale Cherry Chicken

This unique dish is perfect for the holidays—or for any time when you want a slightly more fancy meal!

2 tbsp grapeseed oil

1-1/2 pounds boneless skinless chicken breast

2 tbsp chopped shallots

2 tbsp balsamic vinegar

10oz bag frozen cherries

1 bunch sliced kale leaves, stems discarded

1 tbsp Dijon mustard

2 tbsp olive oil

Pound chicken breast to 1/4 inch thickness with a mallet.

Cook shallots in grapeseed oil for 1 minute on low heat.

Add cherries; cover and cook for 3 minutes more.

Add vinegar, mustard, and kale, and stir to combine.

Cover and cook on low for 5 minutes.

In a separate skillet, cook chicken in olive oil over medium high heat for 5 minutes per side.

Place cooked chicken in skillet with cherry sauce.

Marinate, uncovered, for 3 minutes on low heat.

Serve.

Sweet Lime Chicken

This Southwestern dish is a delicious meal that takes very little time to prepare!

3 tbsp olive oil

1 (3 pound) chicken

1/4 cup agave nectar

3 limes

1 tbsp sea salt

2 onions

1/4 tsp cumin

1 head garlic

1/4 tsp chili powder

Preheat oven to 350 degrees Fahrenheit.

Place chicken, breast side down, in a baking dish and drizzle with olive oil and agave nectar.

Sprinkle with salt, chili powder, and cumin.

Stuff one lime into the chicken cavity, and slice the other two and place around the chicken in the baking dish.

Halve onions and place around chicken in baking dish.

Break garlic head and scatter cloves around chicken in baking dish.

Bake for 45 minutes or until skin begins to brown.

Remove chicken and turn breast side up; increase heat to 450 degrees Fahrenheit.

Bake for 20 minutes more.

Serve drizzled with pan juices.

Apple Rosemary Chicken

Get some fall flavor in your dinners with this easy recipe.

1 (3 pound) chicken

1/4 cup balsamic vinegar

1/4 cup olive oil

1 tbsp olive oil

4 sprigs rosemary

4 cored and sliced apples

Preheat oven to 350 degrees Fahrenheit.

Place chicken in a baking dish, breast side up.

Drizzle with vinegar and oil; sprinkle with salt.

Place apple slices around chicken in baking dish.

Place rosemary underneath the chicken.

Bake for 90 minutes.

Serve.

Conclusion

Thank you again for downloading this book!

I hope this book was able to help you to get educated about a grain-free diet, how it can help you lose weight and get healthy, and how easy it is to prepare delicious grain free meals at any time.

The next step is to start cooking!

www.ingramcontent.com/pod-product-compliance
Lightning Source LLC
Chambersburg PA
CBHW070421190526
45169CB00003B/1363